US ARMED FORCES

JOIN THE AIR FORCE

By P. P. Mitchell

HOT TOPICS

Gareth Stevens Publishing

Please visit our website, www.garethstevens.com. For a free color catalog of all our high-quality books, call toll free 1-800-542-2595 or fax 1-877-542-2596.

Library of Congress Cataloging-in-Publication Data

Names: Mitchell, P. P., author.
Title: Join the Air Force / P. P. Mitchell.
Description: New York : Gareth Stevens Publishing, [2018] | Series: U.S. Armed Forces | Includes index.
Identifiers: LCCN 2016056601| ISBN 9781538205310 (pbk. book) | ISBN 9781538205402 (6 pack) | ISBN 9781538205327 (library bound book)
Subjects: LCSH: United States. Air Force--Juvenile literature. | United States. Air Force--Vocational guidance--Juvenile literature.
Classification: LCC UG633 .M389 2018 | DDC 358.40023/73--dc23
LC record available at https://lccn.loc.gov/2016056601

Published in 2018 by
Gareth Stevens Publishing
111 East 14th Street, Suite 349
New York, NY 10003

Designer: Bethany Perl
Editor: Joan Stoltman

Photo credits: Cover, p. 1 (pilot) Tyler Stableford/Iconica/Getty Images; cover, p. 1 (jet) Chris Parypa Photograhy/Shutterstock.com; cover, 1-32 (camoflage) TravisAF/Wikipedia.org; cover, pp. 1-32 (grunge effect) iulias/Shutterstock.com; cover, pp. 1-32 (rounded text box) foxie/Shutterstock.com; cover, pp. 1-31 (border) jumpingsack/Shutterstock.com; pp. 2-32 (text box) Olga_C/Shutterstock.com; pp. 5-29 (dog tag) Feng Yu/Shutterstock.com; photos courtesy of US Air Force: p. 5 by Master Sgt. Ben Blocker, p. 7 by Staff Sgt. Joe W. McFadden, p. 9 by Airman 1st Class Krystral Ardrey, p. 13 by Airman 1st Class Robert J. Volio, p. 19 by Samuel King Jr., p. 21 by Naoto Anazawa, p. 23 by Senior Airman John Linzmcicr, p. 25 by Tech. Sqt. Manuel J. Martinez, p. 27 by Senior Airman Dana J. Cable, p. 29 by Staff Sgt. Vernon Young Jr., p. 30 by Senior Airman Nicholas Caceres, p. 30 by Airman 1st Class Clayton Cupit; pp. 11, 29 (American Flag) Nataliia K/Shutterstock.com; p. 15 JOSE CABEZAS/AFP/Getty Images; p. 17 iStockphoto.com/casch; p. 30 Glynnis Jones/Shutterstock.com.

Printed in the United States of America

CPSIA compliance information: Batch #CS17GS: For further information contact Gareth Stevens, New York, New York at 1-800-542-2595.

CONTENTS

What's the Air Force All About? 4
What Does an Airman Do? 6
How Do I Join? 10
Special Jobs in the Air Force 20
Airmen in Space 26
How Can I Get Ready Now? 28
For More Information 31
Glossary 32
Index 32

WHAT'S THE AIR FORCE ALL ABOUT?

Joining the US Air Force is a great way to serve your country, have a cool job, and travel! There are 65 bases in the United States and over 20 bases in Europe and Asia. You'll be joining a force of over 313,000 men and women!

DID YOU KNOW?

In the air force, you'll probably move around a lot because different bases, or places where an armed force is, will need your skills and knowledge.

WHAT DOES AN AIRMAN DO?

Anyone in the air force is called an airman. Some airmen are the pilots who fly planes. But there are many other jobs, too! Ground teams help keep aircraft in good working order and do **maintenance**.

DID YOU KNOW?

Even though they're called airmen, women have been in the air force since it formed. They work as pilots, ground crews, nurses, and much more.

Airmen also work in offices, doing jobs like planning aircraft maintenance or ordering safety gear. They may work in communications. Some airmen even work in labs inventing and testing new **technologies** for air travel!

DID YOU KNOW?

For the air force, communications can mean keeping in contact with planes in the air, crews on the ground, or airmen in battle.

HOW DO I JOIN?

There are two paths you can take to join the air force: enlisting or training as an officer. Enlisting means you join and begin work after a little training. Officers train longer and start with a higher rank than enlisted airmen.

AIR FORCE RANKS

OFFICERS

GENERAL OF THE AIR FORCE
GENERAL
LIEUTENANT GENERAL
MAJOR GENERAL
BRIGADIER GENERAL
COLONEL
LIEUTENANT COLONEL
MAJOR
CAPTAIN
FIRST LIEUTENANT
SECOND LIEUTENANT

ENLISTED

CHIEF MASTER SERGEANT OF THE AIR FORCE
COMMAND CHIEF MASTER SERGEANT
CHIEF MASTER SERGEANT
SENIOR MASTER SERGEANT
MASTER SERGEANT
TECHNICAL SERGEANT
STAFF SERGEANT
SENIOR AIRMAN
AIRMAN FIRST CLASS
AIRMAN
AIRMAN BASIC

DID YOU KNOW?

A rank is a title that shows your responsibility, or duty, in the armed forces. There are different names for each rank in every branch of the armed forces.

DID YOU KNOW?

You can enlist at age 17 if a recruiter speaks to your parents and they agree to allow it. A recruiter is the person in your community who helps people enlist in the armed forces.

You can enlist at age 18.

You'll answer questions from a recruiter, then take a test that shows your knowledge, skills, and strengths. Then, they'll test your body. If you pass everything, you can go to basic military training!

SURPRENANT
U.S. AIR FORCE

You can also enlist after you go to school to become a doctor or lawyer. The air force needs people trained in these fields, too! Air force lawyers are called JAGs. They specialize in air and space law, international law, and more!

DID YOU KNOW?

"JAG" is short for "Judge Advocate General." JAGs belong to the Judge Advocate General's Corps, or group, in the air force.

There are several ways to train to be an officer. You can join the Air Force Reserve Officer's Training Corps (AFROTC) at over 1,100 colleges throughout the country. Or you can go to Officer Training School after college.

DID YOU KNOW?

The air force is the youngest military branch in the United States. Before it was formed in 1947, pilots and their crews served in the army.

Graduating from the Air Force Academy in Colorado will also make you an officer. It's a 4-year college. It's so hard to get into that some students start to get ready in middle school!

DID YOU KNOW?

Getting ready as early as middle school means getting good grades by studying and doing your homework and keeping your body healthy and fit.

SPECIAL JOBS IN THE AIR FORCE

Most airmen aren't pilots because it takes a lot of training and skill. To become a pilot, you must first become an officer. Then, flight training takes around 2 years. Pilots need good eyesight. They can't wear glasses or contacts!

DID YOU KNOW?

Having **surgery** to make your eyesight better isn't allowed for air force pilots. You have to be born with good eyesight!

Air Force Special Operations, or Ops, are some of the greatest fighters in the military. Training includes classes on **parachuting** and diving. Special Ops has three different job paths: Combat Control Team (CCTs), Pararescuemen (PJs), and Weather technicians (SOWTs).

DID YOU KNOW?

SOWTs decide when **missions** happen based on the state of weather. They're even trained to tell what the weather could be!

CCTs train for years to decide how to get in and out of land, water, and air missions safely. PJs are airmen trained to parachute, dive, rock climb, and fight to find and save hurt troops.

DID YOU KNOW?

PJs are also trained to perform emergency medicine, the kind of medicine used to treat someone who's been very badly hurt.

AIRMEN IN SPACE

Many early tests about flying and the limits of the human body were done by the air force. This work helped get astronauts into space! Today, thousands of airmen work for the National Aeronautics and Space Administration (NASA).

DID YOU KNOW?

NASA's top **research** center is on Edwards Air Force Base in southern California!

HOW CAN I GET READY NOW?

Do you want to join the air force when you're older? Keep reading about the air force, its history, and past missions. Keep your body and mind in shape. The air force needs people who are prepared, work hard, and will serve with pride.

AIRMAN'S CREED

I am an American airman. I am a warrior. I have answered my nation's call. I am an American airman. My mission is to fly, fight, and win. I am faithful to a proud heritage, a tradition of honor, and a legacy of valor. I am an American airman. Guardian of freedom and justice, my nation's sword and shield, its sentry and avenger. I defend my country with my life. I am an American airman. Wingman, leader, warrior. I will never leave an airman behind, I will never falter, and I will not fail.

DID YOU KNOW?

To be even better prepared for the air force, practice saying the Airman's Creed, the words all airmen live by.

AIR FORCE UNIFORMS

FORMAL UNIFORM

BATTLE UNIFORM

FLIGHT DUTY UNIFORM

FOR MORE INFORMATION

Books

Aronin, Miriam. *Today's Air Force Heroes*. New York, NY: Bearport Publishing, 2012.

Boothroyd, Jennifer. *Inside the US Air Force*. Minneapolis, MN: Lerner Publications, 2017.

Burgan, Michael. *Today's U.S. Air Force*. North Mankato, MN: Compass Point Books, 2013.

Websites

U.S. Air Force
airforce.com
Explore the air force's official website.

Wars and Military History
kids.usa.gov/history/wars/index.shtml
Read all about wars the United States has taken part in.

Publisher's note to educators and parents: Our editors have carefully reviewed these websites to ensure that they are suitable for students. Many websites change frequently, however, and we cannot guarantee that a site's future contents will continue to meet our high standards of quality and educational value. Be advised that students should be closely supervised whenever they access the Internet.

GLOSSARY

maintenance: the labor of fixing something or keeping it in good working shape

mission: a task or job a group must perform

parachute: to drop from an aircraft with a special cloth that slows the fall

research: studying to find something new

surgery: a medical treatment used for conditions and illnesses that involves operations

technology: the way people do something using tools and the tools that they use

INDEX

AFROTC 16
Air Force Academy 18
airmen 6, 7, 8, 20, 24, 26, 29
bases 4, 5
CCTs 22, 24
enlisted airmen 10
JAGs 14
NASA 26, 27
officers 10, 11, 16, 18, 20
Officer Training School 16
pilots 6, 7, 16, 20, 21
PJs 22, 24
rank 10, 11
recruiter 12
SOWTs 22
Special Ops 22
training 10, 12, 20, 22